2016 Coloring Quote Calendar

DOODLE ART ALLEY BOOKS

Samantha Snyder

2016 Coloring Quote Calendar is available at
special discounts when purchased in quantities for
educational use, fundraising, or sales promotions.
For more information, contact: info@akabooks.com

Cover images © 2015 by Doodle Art Alley.

Eleanor Roosevelt quote used with permission.

ISBN-13: 978-0983918271
ISBN-10: 0983918279

This edition is published by aka Associates.
www.akabooks.com

Doodle Art Alley Books

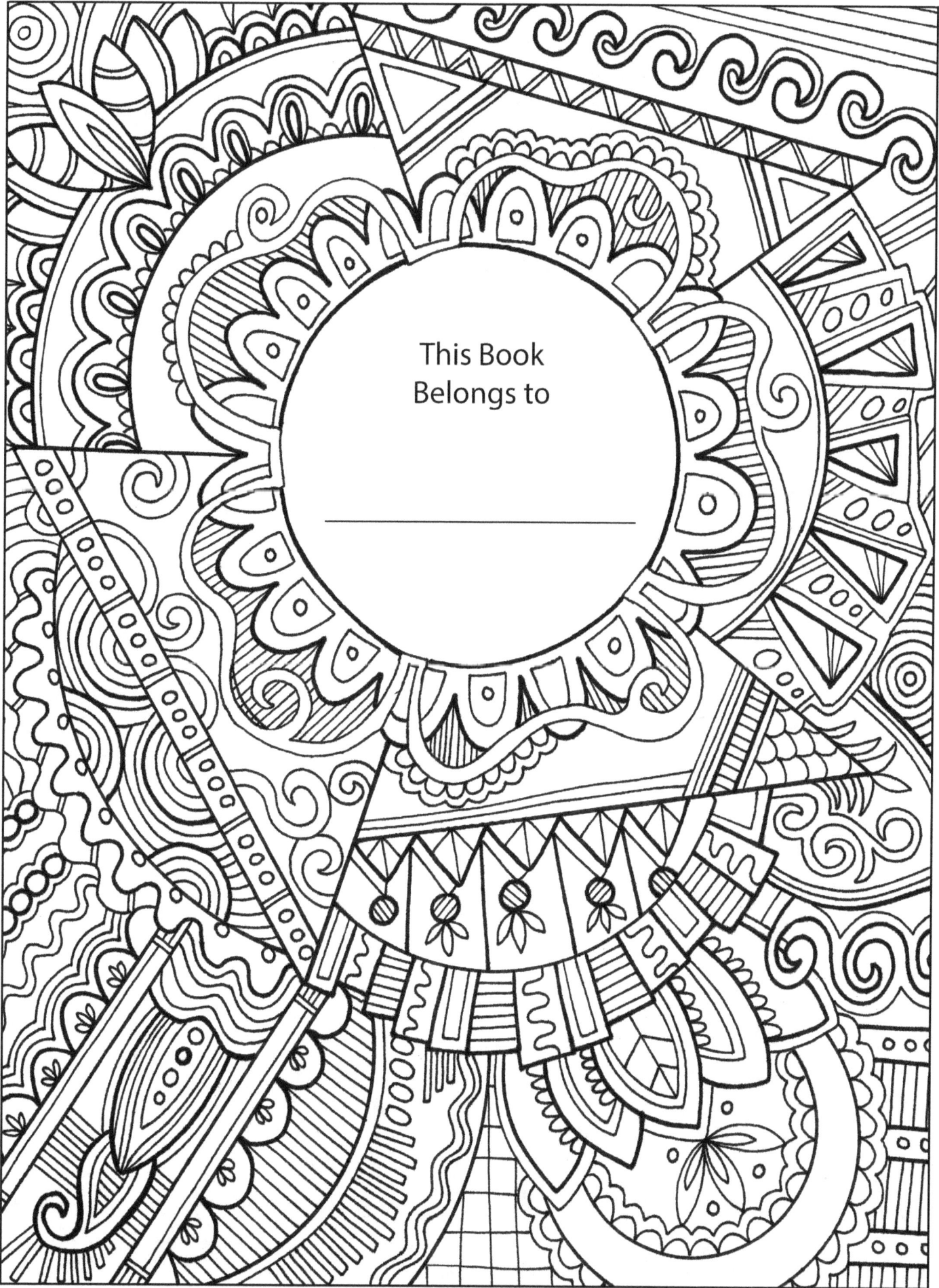

This Book
Belongs to

_____

Charles Dickens

A New Heart for a New Year, Always

January

SUNDAY	MONDAY	TUESDAY	WEDNESDAY	THURSDAY	FRIDAY	SATURDAY
					1	2
3	4	5	6	7	8	9
10	11	12	13	14	15	16
17	18	19	20	21	22	23
24	25	26	27	28	29	30
31						

NOTES

_____

_____

_____

GOALS

_____
_____
_____
_____
_____
_____
_____
_____
_____
_____
_____
_____

EVENTS

_____
_____
_____
_____
_____
_____
_____
_____
_____
_____
_____
_____

MY DOODLES

_____

_____

_____

_____

_____

_____

_____

_____

_____

_____

_____

_____

_____

_____

_____

_____

_____

_____

_____

_____

_____

_____

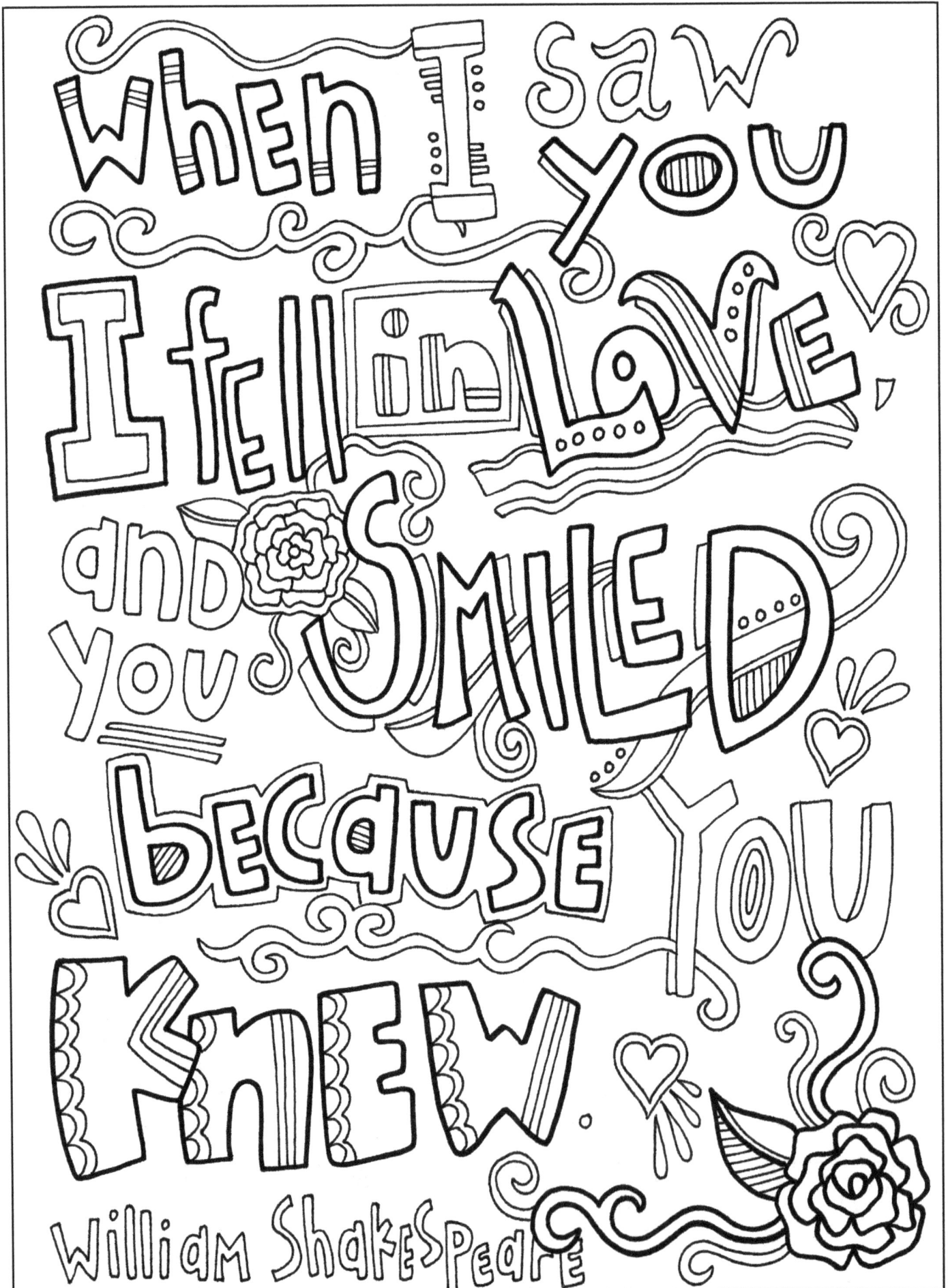

When I saw you I fell in Love, and you Smiled because you Knew.

William Shakespeare

FEBRUARY

SUNDAY	MONDAY	TUESDAY	WEDNESDAY	THURSDAY	FRIDAY	SATURDAY
	1	2	3	4	5	6
7	8	9	10	11	12	13
14	15	16	17	18	19	20
21	22	23	24	25	26	27
28	29					

NOTES

_____

_____

_____

GOALS

_____
_____
_____
_____
_____
_____
_____
_____
_____
_____
_____
_____
_____
_____
_____

EVENTS

_____
_____
_____
_____
_____
_____
_____
_____
_____
_____
_____
_____
_____
_____
_____

MY DOODLES

_____

_____

_____

_____

_____

_____

_____

_____

_____

_____

_____

_____

_____

_____

_____

_____

_____

_____

_____

_____

_____

_____

_____

_____

_____

_____

_____

_____

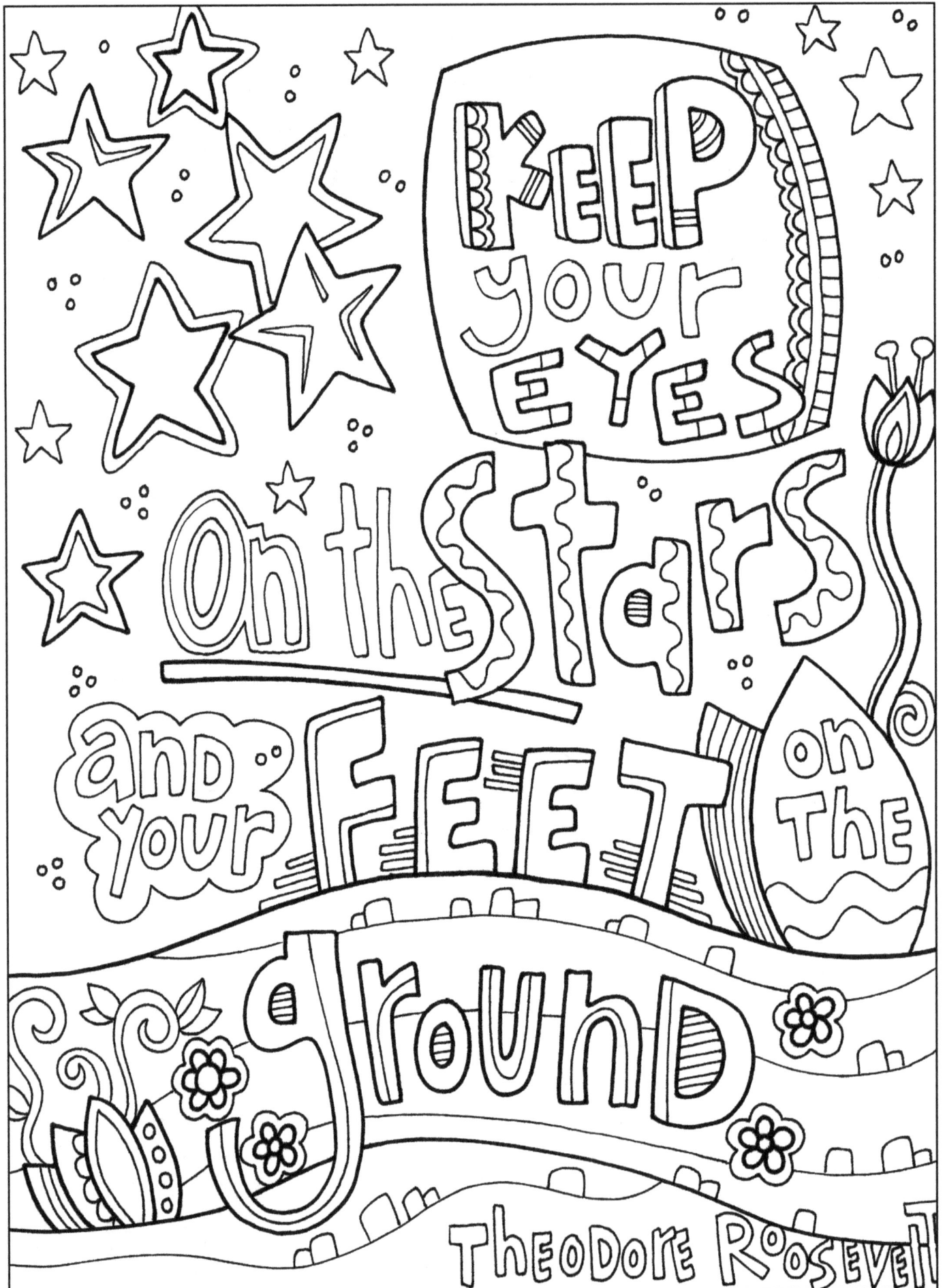

KEEP YOUR EYES ON THE STARS AND YOUR FEET ON THE GROUND

THEODORE ROOSEVELT

March

SUNDAY	MONDAY	TUESDAY	WEDNESDAY	THURSDAY	FRIDAY	SATURDAY
		1	2	3	4	5
6	7	8	9	10	11	12
13	14	15	16	17	18	19
20	21	22	23	24	25	26
27	28	29	30	31		

NOTES

_____

_____

_____

GOALS

_____
_____
_____
_____
_____
_____
_____
_____
_____
_____
_____
_____
_____
_____

EVENTS

_____
_____
_____
_____
_____
_____
_____
_____
_____
_____
_____
_____
_____
_____

MY DOODLES

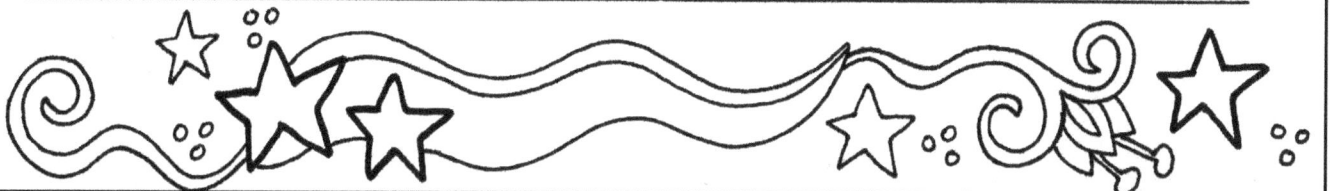

Walt Whitman

Happiness not in another place but this place not for another hour, but this hour.

APRIL

SUNDAY	MONDAY	TUESDAY	WEDNESDAY	THURSDAY	FRIDAY	SATURDAY
					1	2
3	4	5	6	7	8	9
10	11	12	13	14	15	16
17	18	19	20	21	22	23
24	25	26	27	28	29	30

NOTES

_____

_____

_____

GOALS

_____
_____
_____
_____
_____
_____
_____
_____
_____
_____
_____
_____
_____
_____
_____

EVENTS

_____
_____
_____
_____
_____
_____
_____
_____
_____
_____
_____
_____
_____
_____
_____

MY DOODLES

_____
_____
_____
_____
_____
_____
_____
_____
_____
_____
_____
_____
_____
_____
_____
_____
_____
_____
_____
_____
_____
_____
_____
_____
_____
_____
_____
_____

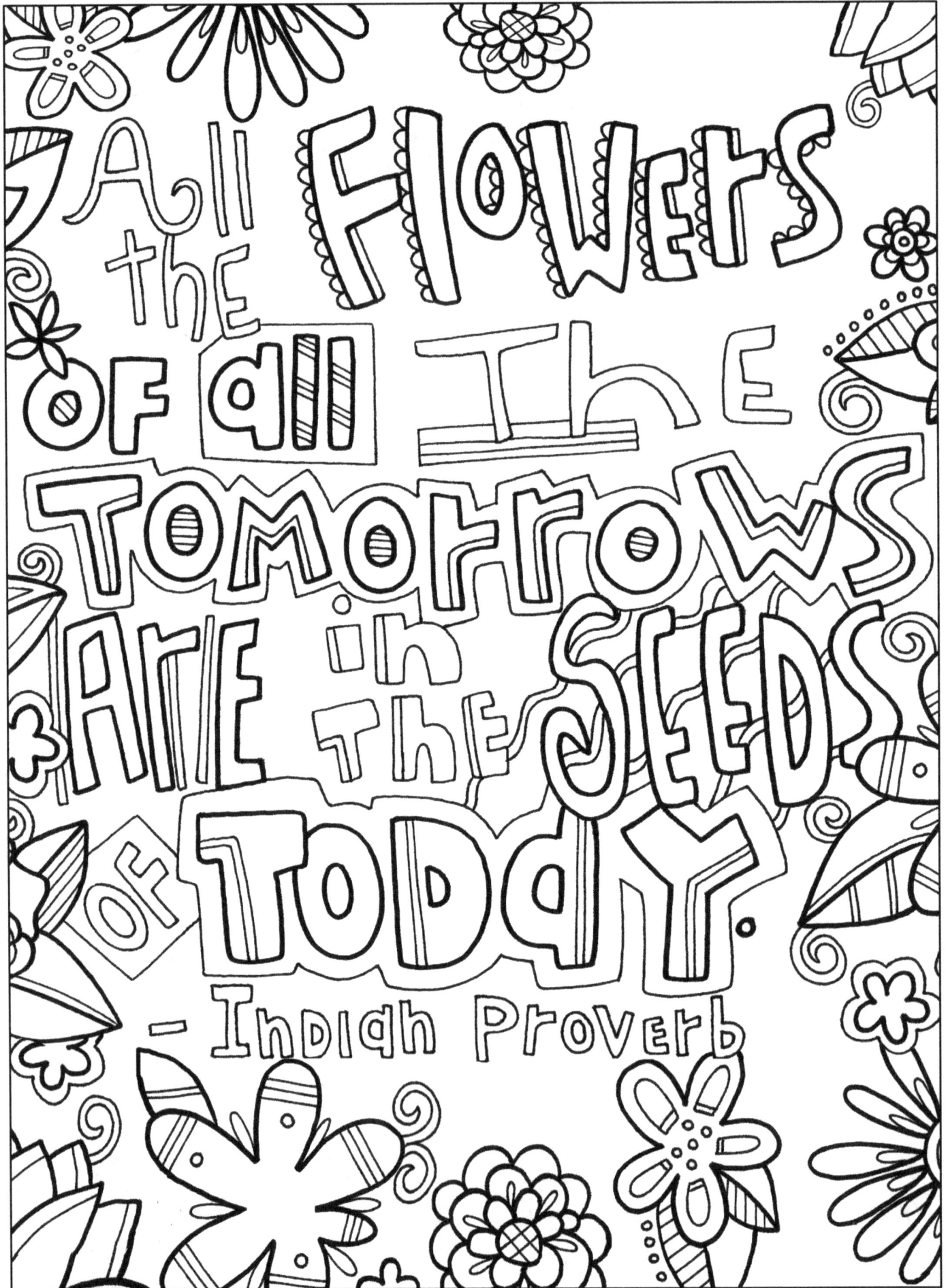

All the Flowers of all The Tomorrows Are in the Seeds of Today.

- Indian Proverb

MAY

SUNDAY	MONDAY	TUESDAY	WEDNESDAY	THURSDAY	FRIDAY	SATURDAY
1	2	3	4	5	6	7
8	9	10	11	12	13	14
15	16	17	18	19	20	21
22	23	24	25	26	27	28
29	30	31				

NOTES

_____

_____

_____

Goals

_____
_____
_____
_____
_____
_____
_____
_____
_____
_____
_____

Events

_____
_____
_____
_____
_____
_____
_____
_____
_____
_____
_____

My Doodles

To Do

A Life without Love is Like A Year without Summer

Swedish Proverb

June

SUNDAY	MONDAY	TUESDAY	WEDNESDAY	THURSDAY	FRIDAY	SATURDAY
			1	2	3	4
5	6	7	8	9	10	11
12	13	14	15	16	17	18
19	20	21	22	23	24	25
26	27	28	29	30		

NOTES

_____

_____

_____

Goals

_____
_____
_____
_____
_____
_____
_____
_____
_____
_____
_____
_____
_____
_____
_____

Events

_____
_____
_____
_____
_____
_____
_____
_____
_____
_____
_____
_____
_____
_____
_____

My Doodles

Just Living is not Enough... One must have Sunshine, Freedom, and a Little Flower

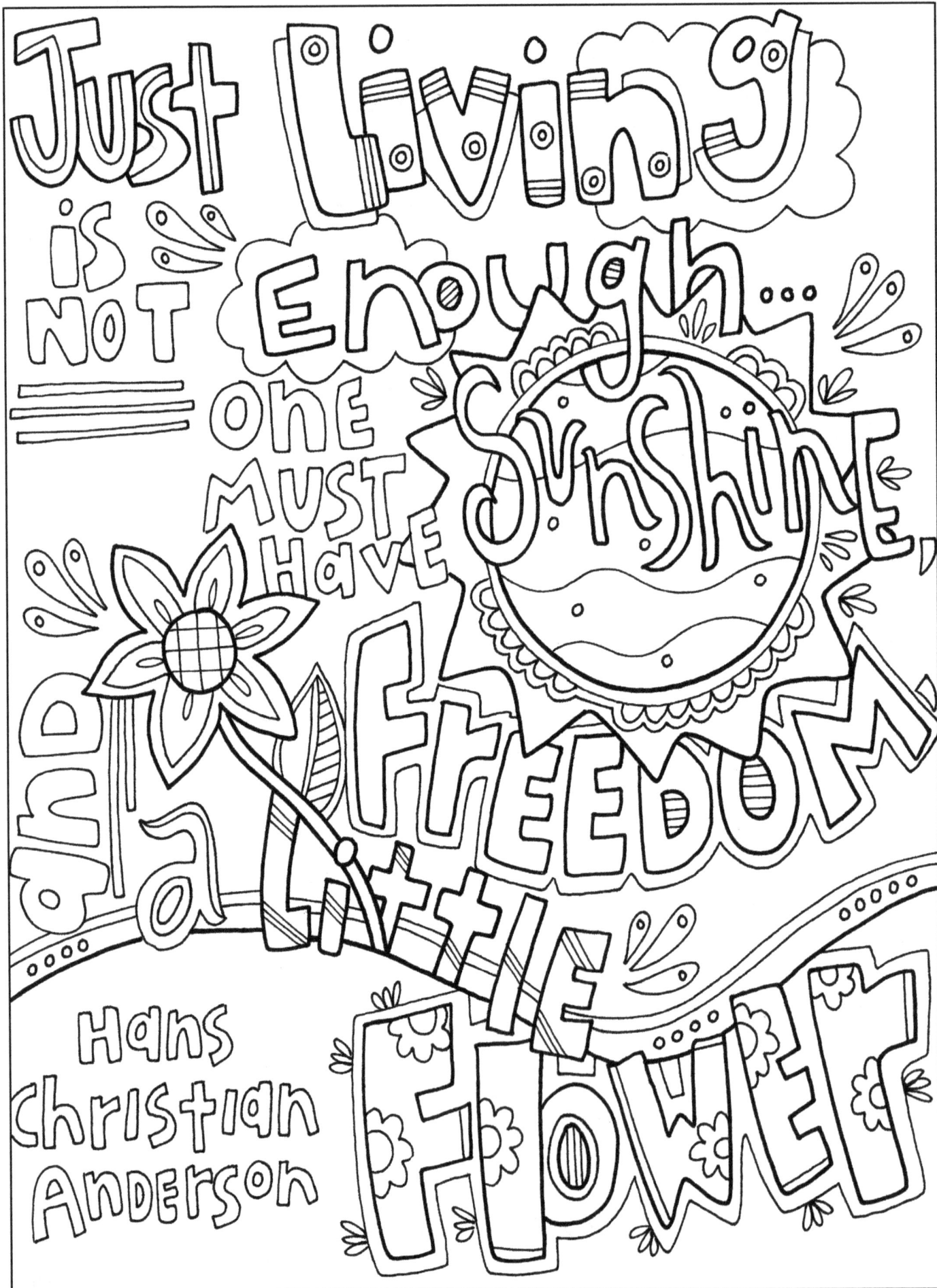

Hans Christian Anderson

JULY

SUNDAY	MONDAY	TUESDAY	WEDNESDAY	THURSDAY	FRIDAY	SATURDAY
					1	2
3	4	5	6	7	8	9
10	11	12	13	14	15	16
17	18	19	20	21	22	23
24	25	26	27	28	29	30
31						

NOTES

_____

_____

_____

GOALS

_____
_____
_____
_____
_____
_____
_____
_____
_____
_____
_____
_____
_____
_____
_____

EVENTS

_____
_____
_____
_____
_____
_____
_____
_____
_____
_____
_____
_____
_____
_____
_____

MY DOODLES

Live in the sunshine, swim in the sea, drink the wild air.

Ralph Waldo Emerson

AUGUST

SUNDAY	MONDAY	TUESDAY	WEDNESDAY	THURSDAY	FRIDAY	SATURDAY
	1	2	3	4	5	6
7	8	9	10	11	12	13
14	15	16	17	18	19	20
21	22	23	24	25	26	27
28	29	30	31			

NOTES

_____

_____

_____

GOALS

_____
_____
_____
_____
_____
_____
_____
_____
_____
_____
_____
_____
_____
_____

EVENTS

_____
_____
_____
_____
_____
_____
_____
_____
_____
_____
_____
_____
_____
_____

MY DOODLES

The World is a Canvas to our Imagination

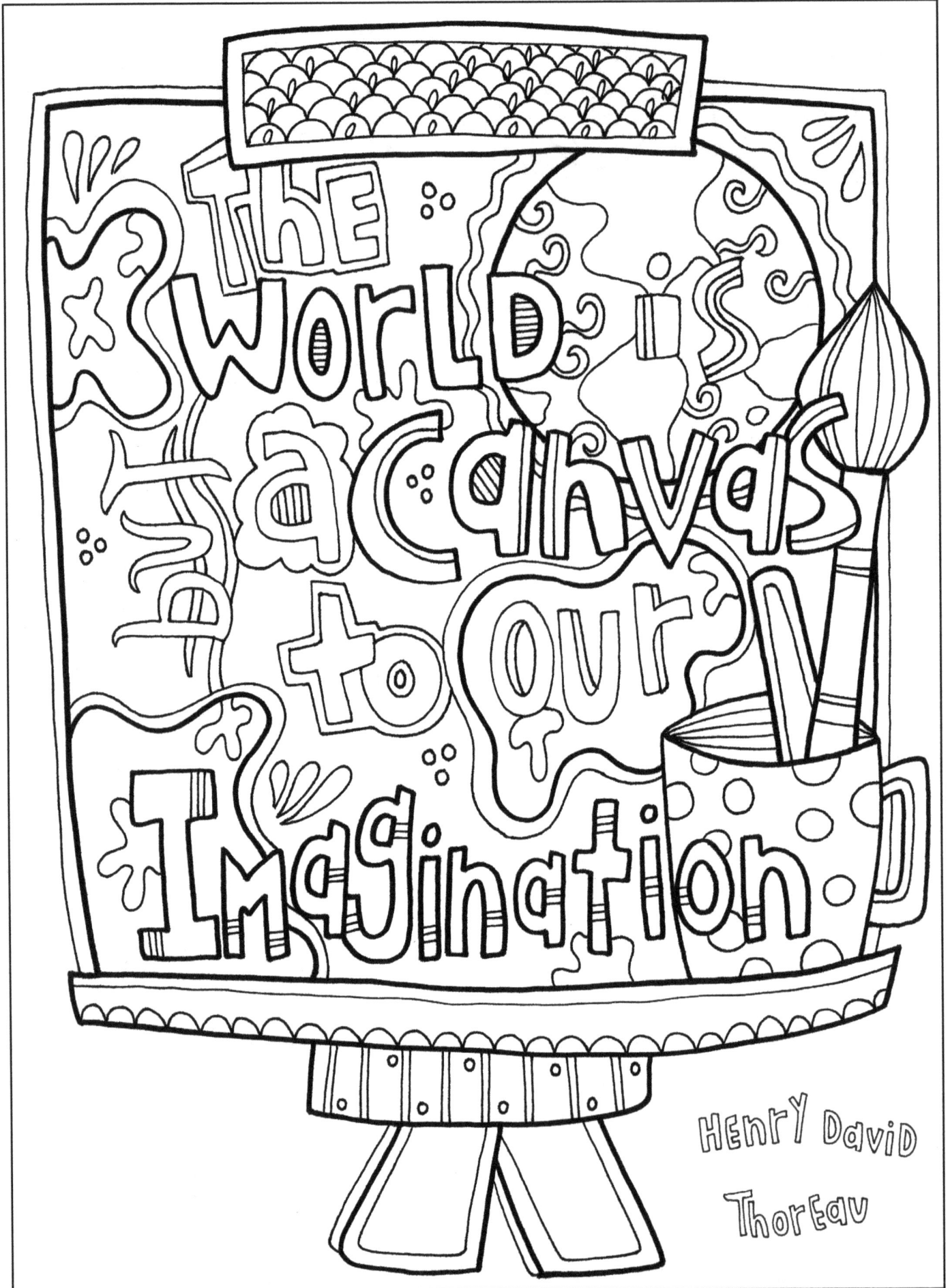

Henry David Thoreau

September

SUNDAY	MONDAY	TUESDAY	WEDNESDAY	THURSDAY	FRIDAY	SATURDAY
				1	2	3
4	5	6	7	8	9	10
11	12	13	14	15	16	17
18	19	20	21	22	23	24
25	26	27	28	29	30	

NOTES

_____

_____

_____

GOALS

_____
_____
_____
_____
_____
_____
_____
_____
_____
_____
_____
_____
_____
_____
_____

EVENTS

_____
_____
_____
_____
_____
_____
_____
_____
_____
_____
_____
_____
_____
_____
_____

MY DOODLES

_____

_____

_____

_____

_____

_____

_____

_____

_____

_____

_____

_____

_____

_____

_____

_____

_____

_____

_____

_____

_____

_____

_____

_____

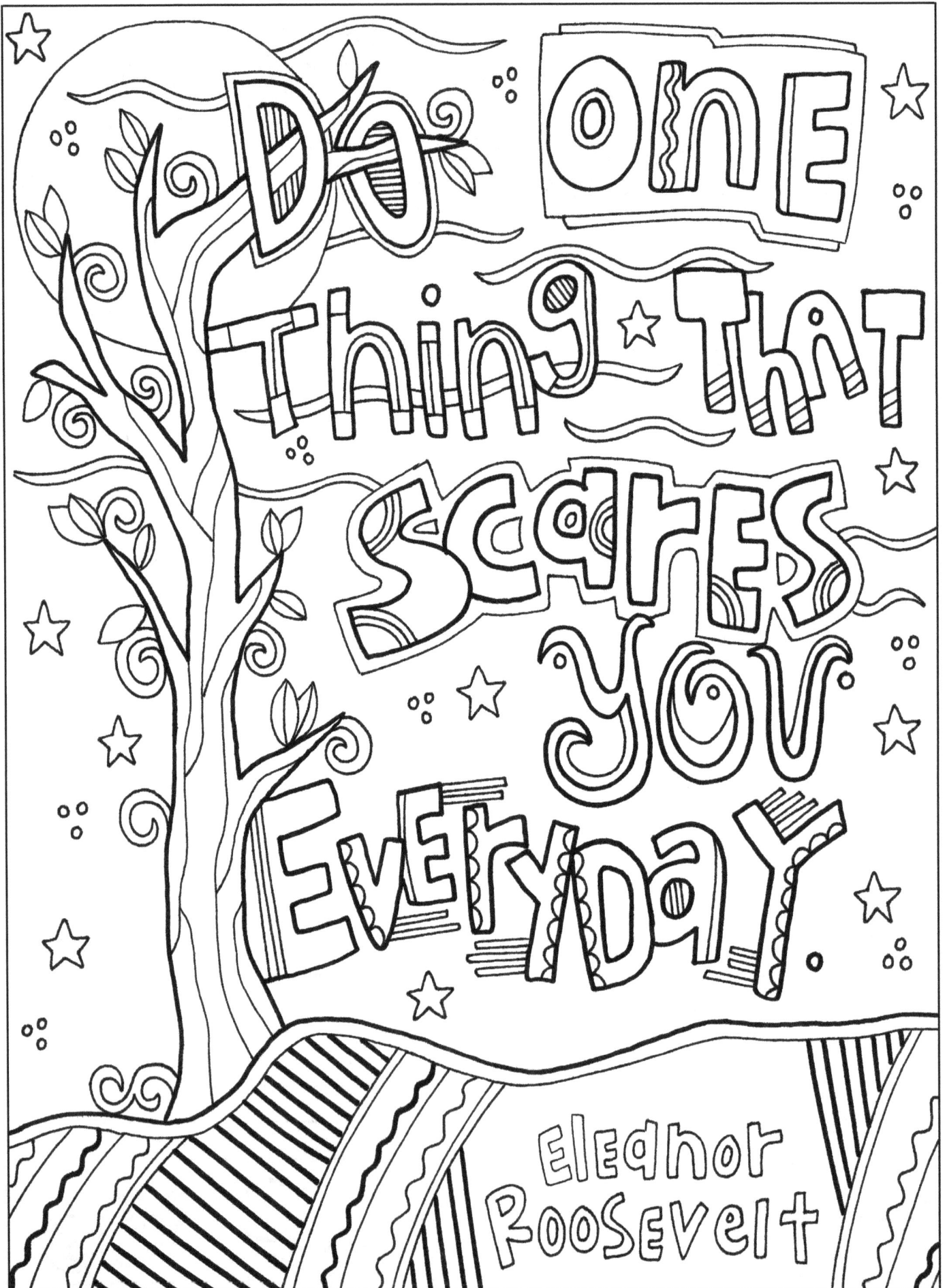

Do one thing that scares you everyday.
Eleanor Roosevelt

OCTOBER

SUNDAY	MONDAY	TUESDAY	WEDNESDAY	THURSDAY	FRIDAY	SATURDAY
						1
2	3	4	5	6	7	8
9	10	11	12	13	14	15
16	17	18	19	20	21	22
23	24	25	26	27	28	29
30	31					

NOTES

_____

_____

_____

GOALS

_____
_____
_____
_____
_____
_____
_____
_____
_____
_____
_____
_____
_____
_____

EVENTS

_____
_____
_____
_____
_____
_____
_____
_____
_____
_____
_____
_____
_____
_____

MY DOODLES

Autumn the year's last loveliest smile

William Cullen Bryant

November

SUNDAY	MONDAY	TUESDAY	WEDNESDAY	THURSDAY	FRIDAY	SATURDAY
		1	2	3	4	5
6	7	8	9	10	11	12
13	14	15	16	17	18	19
20	21	22	23	24	25	26
27	28	29	30			

NOTES

_____

_____

_____

Goals

_____
_____
_____
_____
_____
_____
_____
_____
_____
_____
_____
_____
_____
_____

Events

_____
_____
_____
_____
_____
_____
_____
_____
_____
_____
_____
_____
_____
_____

My Doodles

Let us love winter, for it is the spring of genius

Pietro Aretino

DECEMBER

SUNDAY	MONDAY	TUESDAY	WEDNESDAY	THURSDAY	FRIDAY	SATURDAY
				1	2	3
4	5	6	7	8	9	10
11	12	13	14	15	16	17
18	19	20	21	22	23	24
25	26	27	28	29	30	31

NOTES

_____

_____

_____

GOALS

_____
_____
_____
_____
_____
_____
_____
_____
_____
_____
_____
_____
_____
_____
_____
_____

EVENTS

_____
_____
_____
_____
_____
_____
_____
_____
_____
_____
_____
_____
_____
_____
_____
_____

MY DOODLES

GOALS

_____
_____
_____
_____
_____
_____
_____
_____
_____
_____
_____
_____
_____
_____
_____
_____

EVENTS

_____
_____
_____
_____
_____
_____
_____
_____
_____
_____
_____
_____
_____
_____
_____
_____

MY DOODLES

To Do

I WILL PREPARE AND SOMEDAY MY CHANCE WILL COME.

-Abraham Lincoln

Doodle Art Alley ©

ABOUT DOODLE ART ALLEY

Samantha Snyder has been doodling her whole life. While teaching elementary school, she often drew up coloring pages and printables for her students and fellow teachers. She decided to start sharing her creations and in 2008, Doodle Art Alley was founded.

A quick glance at a doodle may show scribbles, random lines and shapes with no meaning or significance. However, with a little love and direction, these drawings have the potential to compete with some of the best artwork there is!

Doodle Art Alley is dedicated to giving those squiggly lines the proper credit they deserve. Who would have thought that such a small and simple idea could possess so much potential?

There are lots of fun doodle art activities, tips, and information to read through and enjoy. Visit www.doodle-art-alley.com for hundreds of exciting doodles.

Doodle Art Alley Books

www.ingramcontent.com/pod-product-compliance
Lightning Source LLC
Chambersburg PA
CBHW081724270326
41933CB00017B/3293